T0199139

Story of Didong...
A Farm Boy Dreams To Be A Lawyer

A true story about a farm boy who persevered in life and surpassed poverty through education

QUEEN WILHELMINA

queenwilhelmina01@gmail.com

A biography of Judge Candido P. Villanueva (1933-2017). Documented and written by Wilhelmina V. Rubio (Queen Wilhelmina) since April 2013. Illustrations by Pol Villanueva. Dedicated to our father's 80th birthday.

To order additional copies of this book, contact:
Xlibris
844-714-8691
www.Xlibris.com
Orders@Xlibris.com

ISBN: Softcover   978-1-9845-8322-2
          EBook   978-1-9845-8321-5

Print information available on the last page

Rev. date: 11/30/2020

Contents

Prologue

     This is an inspiring story of how a poor farm boy from Dasmarinas, Cavite (Philippines) rose against poverty and adversities in life to fulfill his life's earnest dream of a good education…. Yes, it is a story of first-generation scholar.

     His love for learning and reading became his armor for success in life. Despite their family's financial hardship, he had excelled in all his elementary, secondary, and college studies while self-supporting himself as an artist-illustrator, and later as a court messenger. He reached his goals through sheer determination and strong faith in God. He later pursued his Doctor of Laws while working as a court stenographer. He realized his dream to become a lawyer in 1959. He was initially appointed as City Fiscal in Cavite City, then later as Department of Justice State Prosecutor. In 1980, he was appointed as Court Judge, and served under the term of five (5) presidents in the Philippines. Here's the incredible life story of Judge Candido P. Villanueva…

His Childhood Years On The Farm

At his early childhood school-local dialect under Mrs. Bautista (Didong is seated on the front row, sixth person from the left)

Candido Purificacion Villanueva was born on October 3, 1933, in the small town of San Agustin, Dasmarinas, Cavite (Philippines). ***Didong***, as he was fondly called, came from a family of farmers and traders *(magsasaka and mangangalakal in Tagalog)*. His parents, four (4) brothers, and four (4) sisters were all farmers. Every day, at the break of dawn, he and his brothers would till the farmland with the able help of a *carabao* (or water buffalo). During harvest season, they picked all their vegetable crops such as okra, eggplant, *sitao* (string beans), bellpeppers, and *ampalaya* (bitter melon), packed them in plastic bags, and sold them to market traders at Divisoria which is the biggest flea market at the center of Manila.

He rode with delivery trucks of vegetables because he was curious and wanted to see Manila, the big city. During deliveries, they carried heavy sacks of vegetables on their backs and unloaded them at the market site. After long hours of unloading, he and his brothers slept on the *bangketas* (sidewalks) of Divisoria market . In their free time, they played and jumped around piles of rice sacks which served as their playground.

Growing up on the farm was fun, however, it was hard and back breaking. They all helped with farming, and putting food on the table. ***"We're eight (8) children of Hermogenes Villanueva and Melencia Purificacion, and I am the 7th child. From the eldest they were: Felisa, Gregoria, Concepcion, Aurea, Felimon, Francisco, and Eduardo."***

"My father was a small farmer-tenant of the Tirona-Benitez family of Imus. But it seems he was a born leader because he became a Teniente del Barrio of San Agustin (elected village leader), where we reside, and later he was elected Municipal Councilor of Dasmarinas, the position he held until his death." At a tender age of 5 , his family struggled from the loss of their father from lung illness (April 12, 1938). His mother Melencia carried the burden of raising all eight (8) children by herself through farming and trading.

"My mother had not gone to school but at least she could sign her name, and with inborn talent, she can compute, add, and subtract. She was able to work as merchant of vegetables. She purchased from farmers and sold them in Santo Cristo Street and Divisoria."

On his 6th Grade, Class 1946-1947 at Dasmariñas Elementary School, where he graduated as Valedictorian. (Didong is on third row standing fourth from left)

In time, Didong realized that farming and vegetable trading was not for him. He got bored with the endless routinary work. He told himself that ***"if I don't study, I will be doing farming for the rest of my life….but I wanted to be able to do something else."*** Unlike his siblings, he found joy and excitement in learning new things at school, as well as in reading history books, comics, and newspapers. Each day, he walked to school barefooted or in beaten up slippers, just to be at school because there he can read his favorite books about the history of the Philippines, and the lives of national heroes.

Despite their family's struggles, Didong continued to study hard. He loved to read not only about his own country, but also about the history of great nations such as United States and Great Britain, biographies of famous forefathers and presidents, the world revolutions, famous English novels, and a lot more. He always helped his classmates with school work, and finished at the top of his class at each grade level. On his 6th grade, Didong graduated as the class Valedictorian at the Dasmarinas Elementary School (DES).

His High School Years

Didong knew he had to work his way through high school because of their family's financial hardships. Since he possessed creative hands, he found a job as an artist-illustrator for designing Christmas cards.

"My mother could not afford the P10 (or $5, based on $1-P2 exchange rate that year) monthly tuition in 1st year of high school. But upon working in the art studio of Mr. Duschane, he took care of my tuition fees at the Infant Jesus Academy, where I finished 1st honor."

He drew and designed greeting cards for a famous artist who sold them to the Department of Philippine Education in Manila. To earn additional income, he likewise worked as dispatcher for *jeepney*s (a public transportation which can sit 10-12 persons).

Didong was unfazed by the challenges in his life. He kept his deep faith in God. He grew up to be a religious young man. Like his mother and sisters, he regularly went to church and attended Sunday Mass. He observed that only the affluent people sat at the front rows so he sat along the side of the church's benches because he knew that they were poor.

Didong studied harder to get good grades so he did not have to pay any tuition fees on his 2nd year and 3rd year high school, at Immaculate Concepcion Academy. He worked hard and garnered the top honors in all his secondary years. ***"When I don't understand my assignment, I read it again the second time, so I can better comprehend it."***

"I was self-supporting in my entire student life from 1st-year high school….Up until my law studies, I was a working student."

One of his fervent wishes was to be able to study in Manila, so he could become familiar with the big city and continue his college education there. On his 4th year in high school, he convinced his mother and sister Aurea, to help him financially with his studies in Manila.

Good enough, he was able to enroll in 4th-year high school at the University of Santo Tomas (UST), considered the oldest and prestigious school in the Philippines, where national hero Dr. Jose Rizal studied. He stayed with a family relative at Prudencio St., in Sampaloc, Manila, which is just a 15-minute walk to UST. While living there, their mean family relative tried to hide food away from him, he had nothing to eat. They also packed and hid his beddings so he had nowhere to sleep.

He finished 4th year high school at University of Sto Tomas,
a prestigious school in the Philippines, so he can continue his college education in the city.

These trials did not deter him from achieving his goals. Fortunately, a good neighbor across his boarding house offered him free board and lodging up until he finished his high school.

After he graduated from high school on March 17, 1951, he decided to study steno typing for six (6) months at Gregg Business College to prepare himself for any future job because he knew that he had to work his way through college. And this will also prepare him for any future job because he believed in the saying that: "Opportunity only comes to those who are well-prepared (and ready to take advantage of it)." (B.C. Flores)

His personal collection of classic novels, law books, and encyclopedias

To accomplish this, he needed to ride the bus back and forth Cavite -Manila en route (42 kilometers or 26 miles, 2-3 hours depending on traffic). To catch Cavite's Saulog bus, he walked from Soler to Avenida, then to Escolta, and waited standing in line at Juan Luna Street. Along his route, he stopped by the United States Information Service (USIS) library of different encyclopedias and books. He enjoyed every minute spent on reading these resources; he promised to himself to acquire the same books once he gets a good job.

"One day I would love to own a complete set of the same encyclopedias and books…."

His first favorite quote:

"The mind, once stretched by a new idea, never returns to its original dimensions."

Attributed to Ralph Waldo Emerson and cited by - Robert Hutchins (Past President of University of Chicago)

His Life's Turning Point

Didong thought that it will be impossible for him to pursue his college education due to his dire financial situation. But he kept his faith and continued to pray for a job that will support him in his college studies. And by twist of fate, God paved the way for him to obtain his degree.

On December 30, 1951, he was selected by high school teachers in Dasmarinas to deliver a speech before thousands of people at their town hall. His declamation speech were excerpts taken from El Filibusterismo, a novel written by Philippine national hero, Dr. Jose Rizal, about the youth as the hope of the land. (See pages 28-29 on the excerpts of his declamation speech in Tagalog and English versions). The day marked the oath-taking of newly elected Governor Dominador M. Camerino and Mayor Emiliano Dela Cruz who were under the Liberal Party.

"They prepared a big stage at the side of the church's plaza and there were more than 5,000 people who attended that program during my speech (declamation)..."

Impressed by his speech, Governor Camerino approached him later and asked: *"If I give you a job, would you want to continue your studies?"*

To which he replied: *"Yes sir, that's what I've been praying for."*

Didong was an active member of their town's youth group. (He is seated on the front row, third from left.)

The job offered by the Governor enabled Didong to enroll in college. On January 2, 1952, at age 18, he started working as a court messenger at the Provincial City Fiscal Office, Cavite Capitol receiving a salary of P90 ($45)/month or P3/day. He worked as a messenger in the morning while pursuing his college studies at night.

Then in 1954, he took and passed the Civil Service examination for government employees. Soon, he was able to apply his steno typing skills when he got promoted to Junior Court Stenographer at the Court of First Instance (CFI) office of Judge Antonio Lucero. He earned P150 ($75)/month and offered legal transcripts to lawyers for a fee.

In the same year, he decided to pursue his big dream of enrolling in Bachelor of Laws at the Francisco Law School. There he met his best friend lawyer, Atty. Raymundo Beltran. After successfully finishing his college degree, he then pursued his Doctor of Laws (LLB) at the Far Eastern University, College of Laws.

"Opportunity only comes to those who are well prepared." (and ready to take advantage of it.)

- By B.C. Forbes

Passing the Bar Examination for Lawyers

At age 25, Didong finally realized his dream to be a lawyer. With dedication and discipline, he passed the tough Bar licensure examination given by the Philippine Supreme Court on April 30, 1959, with a score of 77.55%.

It was the most memorable day of his life, and he felt all of his hardships had finally paid off. He excitedly went home to his mother to tell her the good news. The bus ride took 4 hours long; it was already dark when he arrived in Dasmarinas. He saw his mother waiting at the porch on her rocking chair and praying.

"Nanay (mother), I am now a lawyer." When he told her the good news she cried. His whole family was so proud of him, for being the first lawyer in their town. He proudly carried the title **Attorney Candido P. Villanueva**.

His sign board at front porch of their old house where people line up for free legal consultation

The next morning, he and his mother went to church to offer thanksgiving mass. Then on May 9, 1959, he took his oath as a lawyer.

"When I passed the bar exam, my family was treated for dinner at the Pagoda restaurant by my then boss, Judge Francisco Geronimo."

Didong is seated in the middle of front row. To his right are his mother Melencia and and Lourdes, his girlfriend at that time.

He made a promise to assist his poor townmates who were treated unjustly or wrongly persecuted by providing them with free or pro bono legal advice. Every weekend when he visits his hometown, there is a long line of people waiting at their porch who needs legal advice. In return, the people felt gratitude for his free legal advice, and offered him sacks of rice, live chickens, a bunch of bananas, and other produce.

His personal life

After he became a lawyer, he married his lovely co-worker, Lourdes Dungca, who also worked as a court stenographer at the same judicial court. They got married at the historic Quiapo, Manila Catholic church on November 12, 1960. They had six children, Victoria (doctor), Wilhelmina (teacher), Alexander (court sheriff), Napoleon (architect), Samson (lawyer), and Emmanuel (engineer). He named his children after famous kings and queens. He has a sharp memory for he memorized the exact date and year of birth of all his children.

After passing the bar, he married his co-worker Lourdes Dungca,
from Cavite City, and they raised six (6) children.

Eventually, Didong resigned as a court stenographer and worked as one of the assistant attorneys at the law offices of former Senator Vicente J. Francisco, one of the most successful practicing lawyers in 1959. After seven (7) years of law practice, he got appointed as assistant provincial fiscal in Cavite City.

Appointed As State Prosecutor, Then As Court Judge

In 1973, he was appointed as Senior State Prosecutor under the Department of Justice in Taft, Manila. In 1980, because of his hard work and integrity, he was appointed by then President Ferdinand Marcos as a Court of First Instance (CFI) Judge of Malolos, Bulacan (a town 20 miles north of Manila).

When he was appointed as Senior State Prosecutor, he took his oath before Secretary Ricardo Puno of the Department of Justice; his mother in a traditional filipiñana gown.

After a few years, he was promoted as Regional Trial Court (RTC) Judge of Makati City, the financial capital of the Philippines. He served under the term of five (5) presidents of the Philippines, namely, President Ferdinand Marcos, Corazon Aquino, Fidel Ramos, Joseph Estrada, and Gloria Macapagal.

In 1980, he took oath as a court judge before then President Ferdinand Marcos.

Makati Regional Trial Court Judges (Judge Didong in the middle standing, third row)

He was elected the president of the Philippines Retired Judges Association in 2014.

His Community Service And Legacy

Formed the Holy Name Society of Phils. – Dasmarinas Chapter

Didong promised to serve God and the church once he becomes a full-fledged lawyer. In the past, he observed that people who comes to church were mostly women, hence, on November 18, 1959, he and Bro. Domeng Genoveo formed the Holy Name Society- Dasmarinas Chapter. "We thought of establishing the HNS to involve the men (young and old) in church activities and faith formation to preserve the family values in our community. Part of our outreach programs is to help those who are poor in riches or poor in spirit." Two years after it was founded, his first child Victoria was born on the same date, November 18, 1961. Didong collaborated with church leaders, priests, and nuns on HNS projects such as feeding programs/food donations, and visiting orphanages, prison inmates and rape victims. Since then, a lot of men have become involved in Christian activities because of HNS. It recently celebrated its 60th year of existence.

His list of organizations:

- Holy Name Society of the Philippines-Dasmarinas Chapter - Founder
- Rotary Club of Dasmarinas, Cavite - Member
- Philippine Retired Judges Association - Past President
- Cofradia de Jesus Nazareno (Cavite City) - Past Hermano Mayor
- Knights of Columbus (Grand Knight)

In 1983, he was awarded Most Outstanding Citizen of Dasmarinas, Cavite by the Sanggunian Bayan ng Dasmarinas (City Council), during its foundation day.

A passionate book collector

All his life, Didong did not waver in his passion for books and in reading (books, Bible, Time and Newsweek magazines, Reader's Digest) his favorite pass time. He had built his very own personal library, a collection of prestigious books that he purchased through installment plans.

He took pride of his grand collection of books which includes:

- Harvard Classic novels,
- Complete set of the Philippine Supreme Court (SCRAA) law books,
- Complete set of Encyclopedia Britannica, and
- Writings of Great Novelists & Writers of Western Civilization (54 Volumes) published by University of Chicago & Encyclopedia Britannica.

On the writings of great novelists, Didong mentioned that: *"It has the writings starting from Homer, and also poems by Longfellow."*

He recalled Robert Hutchins, president of University of Chicago, wrote the introduction for the Great Novelists book, and he gave this quote: *"The mind, once stretched by a new idea, never returns to its original dimensions."*

Didong also recalled what Mortimer J. Adler, editor of Great Novelists, said in his article on "Great Ideas from the Great Books" where he wrote about the **"Element of Chances in Human Life"**. Adler stated that most American theologians agree with St. Augustine when he said: *"Nothing happens at random in this world...Everything, even what happens by chance, is a will of God."* This he said could refer to our marriages and friendships we have nurtured in our lives.

Didong became a widower at the age 61, and remarried Amelia Ignacio, also a widow, on June 21, 1996. After 23 years as a judge, he retired from judiciary practice compulsory at age of 70 in 2003. He devoted his retirement years to community services, traveling, spending time with family and twelve (12) grandchildren, and socializing with other co-retired judges. In 2014, he was elected the president of the Philippine Retired Judges Association.

He passed away and joined His Creator on a summer day, July 2nd of 2017, at the age of 83. At his wake, His Eminence Cardinal Luis Antonio Tagle and Bishop Pedro Arigo came to give their respects. From his humble beginnings, Didong lived a fruitful life that was rooted on perseverance, deep faith in God, and service. He worked hard to achieve his dream, excelled in his law profession, and made a difference in people's lives. Overall, his life journey can be summed up in his last favorite quote:

"Nothing happens at random in this world...Everything, even what happens by chance, is a will of God."

**- By St. Augustine
(Cited by Mortimer J. Adler,
editor of Great Novelists in his article on
"Element of Chances in Human Life")**

With Didong's dedicated service to the church and the community, Cardinal Luis Antonio Tagle and Bishop Pedro Arigo gave their respects at his wake at the Sacred Heart Memorial Gardens (Dasmarinas, Cavite).

Timeline Of His Achievements As A Lawyer:

1959 – Became a lawyer; worked as Asst. Attorney with pay of P250/month.

1967 – Worked under the government, appointed as Acting 4th Asst. Provincial Fiscal of Cavite City (at the same office where he worked as clerk messenger); then promoted to 1st Asst. Provincial Fiscal

1973 – Appointed Senior State Prosecutor under the Department of Justice (DOJ), Manila

1975 – Government representative to the United Nations Asia and Far East Institute for the Prevention of Crimes and Treatment of Offenders (UNAFEI), a Colombo Plan scholarship grant, held in Tokyo, Japan

1976 – Awarded as Outstanding Government Prosecutor by DOJ, Manila

1980 – Appointed as Court of First Instance (CFI) Judge in Malolos, Bulacan (north of Manila)

1987 – Appointed as Regional Trial Court (RTC) Judge in financial district Makati City

1983 – Awarded Most Outstanding Citizen of Dasmarinas, Cavite by the Sangguniang Bayan ng Dasmarinas, during its foundation day.

1987 – Government representative to the Academy of American and International Law, a fellowship grant, held in Dallas, Texas

2003 – Didong retired as a judge at the compulsory age of 70.

In 1987, Didong was also the government representative to the Academy of the American and International Law, a fellowship grant held in Dallas, Texas, USA. (Didong is standing on the front row, third person from the right).

The author with her aunt Aurea in traditional farming attire.

Didong on his 75th birthday with his family and sisters Aurea and Concepcion.

"Youth, the Hope of the Land"

Didong delivered his declamation speech on the youth as the hope of the land at their city of Dasmarinas' town hall before a crowd of thousands of people. He used excerpts from El Filibusterismo (in Tagalog), one of the popular revolutionary novels written by national hero, Dr. Jose Rizal. Right after his speech, he was offered a job by then Cavite Governor Camerino which enabled him to pursue his dream of college education.

"Kabataan, Ang Pag-Asa Ng Bayan"

(Tagalog Version)

"Nasaan ang mga kabataan na dapat ilaan ang kanilang gintuang mga oras, ang kanilang mga ilusyon at sigasig para sa kabutihan ng bayan?

Nasaan ang mga ito na dapat nang bukas-palad paaagusin ang kanilang dugo upang hugasan palayo sa labis na kahihiyan, maraming mabibigat na kasalanan, labis na pagkasuklam?

Tapat, mga dalisay at walang bahid-dungis na biktima para kahirapan ay maging katanggap-tanggap.

Nasaan ka, kayo ang mga anak na dapat isama ang mga lakas ng buhay na ay tumakas mula sa iyong mga ugat, ang kadalisayan ng mga ideya na ito ay naging sa ating isipan at ng apoy ng sigla na ay nawala sa ating mga puso?

Kami ay naghihintay sa iyo, Oh kabataan!

Darating, kami ay naghihintay sa inyo!"

"Youth, The Hope Of The Land"

(English Version)

"Where are the young who must dedicate their roseate hours, their illusions and enthusiasm to the good of the country?

Where are they who must generously spill their blood to wash away so much shame, so many crimes, so much abomination?

Pure and spotless must be the victim for the holocaust to be acceptable.

Where are you, you children who must embody the vigor of life that has fled from your veins, the purity of ideas that has become in our minds and the fire of enthusiasm that has gone out in our hearts?

We await you, Oh youth! Come, we await you!"

- Excerpts from famous revolutionary poem El Filibusterismo by Philippine national hero, Dr. Jose Rizal

Judge Candido P. Villanueva (Ret.) .....Husband, Father, Lawyer, Fiscal, State Prosecutor, Farmer, Valedictorian, Leader, Priest (almost), Artist, Public Speaker (Excellent), Grand Knight, Holy Namer, Rotarian, Lay Minister, Writer, and a Proud Grandfather (of 12 Grandchildren)......

References

www.pixabay.com

www.pexels.com

www.unsplash.com

www.ust.edu.ph

www.goodreads.com/quotes

www.inspiringquotes.us/authors

www.googletranslate.com

Afterword From Author

To our beloved Daddy Judge, thank you for the unconditional love, guidance, and life lessons you taught us. We are blessed to have you us our father.

We have always been inspired by your humble beginnings, thus we love retelling your life story to the younger generations citing the value of education, family values, and serving the community. You have shown us that anyone can possibly achieve his dream despite setbacks in life by working hard on one's goal, and by keeping a strong faith in God.

(Part of the proceeds from the sale of this book will be used to continue with Judge Candido P. Villanueva's legacy on faith formation, helping the community, and assisting the less fortunate students.)

JUDGE CANDIDO PURIFICACION VILLANUEVA

03 OCTOBER 1933 - 02 JULY 2017

Printed in the United States
By Bookmasters